Cold Soup

Nic Aubury

Nasty Little Press

Published by Nasty Little Press in July 2013.

Nasty Little Press
35 St Johns Road, Bungay, Suffolk, NR35 1DH
nastylittlepress.org | @nastylit

ISBN: 978-0-9573000-5-7

Set in Book Antiqua.
Printed and bound by Berforts Information Press Ltd.

A CIP rec[ord] [is available]
from the [British Library.]

Cover illu[stra]tion by Sam Ratcliffe.

For my wife

Contents

COLD SOUP

True Inspiration

It isn't that I feel compelled to sing of mankind's woes,
or lament the tragic brevity of life;
and it isn't that I long to tell of victory over foes,
or the conquest of another fellow's wife;
and it isn't that my heart's ablaze with unrequited love,
or my spirit stirred by some enchanted view;
I've been moved to write this poem as a way of putting off
the annoying list of things I've got to do.

Otherwise

The owl is not the wisest bird,
in spite of what you might have heard,
for, if he were, I think - don't you? –
he'd say 'Too whoom' and not 'Too whoo'.

Good Gran, Bad Gran

Good gran had dimples and hair in a bun;
bad gran had gout and a whiskery beard.
Good gran told stories and loved having fun;
bad gran was grumpy and smelled a bit weird.
Good gran made biscuits and flapjacks and treats;
bad gran made liver and onions with mash.
Good gran gave 50p pieces for sweets;
bad gran had tins, which she hid, full of cash.
Good gran had cupboards of marbles and games;
bad gran had varicose veins and a cough.
Good gran had goldfish with humorous names;
bad gran drank sherry, and then nodded off.
Good gran had hats topped with tropical fruits;
bad gran had nets that she wore on her head.
Good gran was caught nicking lipstick from Boots;
 'It's never the ones you'd expect', bad gran said.

Feeder

A fry-up, then elevenses;
a Sunday roast, then tea.
By god, she puts the 'hospital'
in 'hospitality'.

Child of Our Times

Monday's child is on the phone.
Tuesday's child would like a loan.
Wednesday's child is underdressed.
Thursday's child is *so*, like, stressed.
Friday's child likes gaming and tweeting.
Saturday's child has issues with eating.
And the child who's born on the Sabbath day
is not a bloody *kid*, OK?

Nine Lives Too Many

Don't look upon your cat with
any fondness, I entreat you.
It's looking back and thinking:
'Were I bigger, I would eat you'.

RSVP

It seems that you like me enough that you'd ask me
to buy you a coffee machine,
or a wall-mounted clock, or a new iPod dock,
or a Villeroy and Boch figurine;
enough that you'd ask for a Waterford vase
or a full set of white, cotton bedding,
but not quite enough that you'd actually like me
to come to the whole of your wedding.

Golden Wedding

They've talked and laughed for fifty years,
no arguments or confrontations,
simply having one half each
of two quite separate conversations.

For Starters

Gazpacho, borscht and vichyssoise
elicit reverent *ooh là là*s
in gourmet restaurants and the homes
of all discerning gastronomes.
To me, a boorish nincompoop,
whatever name you give cold soup,
there's nothing to redeem it, save
a minute in the microwave.

The Waistband

April? No, I disagree.
The cruellest month is January.

The Morning After

Adam woke up, and then Eve did the same
(though neither remembered the other one's name).
'Good morning. Did we…?' and his voice trailed off.
'I think so' she said with a shy little cough.
'Well, all I remember' he said, sounding jumpy,
'was downing that snakebite and horrible scrumpy,
but everything else after that's just a blur',
and she said that things were the same way for her.
'And these fig leaves?' asked Adam, now edging to leave.
'I haven't the faintest idea' replied Eve.

In Praise of Family Life

Despite what inveterate bachelors claim
are the drawbacks of children and wives,
at least those who have them have someone to blame
for how little they've made of their lives.

Cornucopia

Assorted batteries (some old, some new);
a nine amp fuse; a ball of bright blue string;
a rawl plug and a one-inch phillips screw;
a heart-shaped, plastic Christmas cracker ring;
a bouncy ball made out of rubber bands;
two bendy drinking-straws (one green, one blue);
a strapless wrist-watch missing both its hands;
a squeezed and dried-up tube of superglue;
the charger for a long-lost mobile 'phone;
a dozen matches in a flattened box;
the label from a decent Côtes du Rhône;
the keys to fit as many unknown locks.
All sorts of stuff lives in my kitchen drawer -
but somehow never what I'm looking for.

Lines Composed in a Drawing Room

Were this furniture magically able
to answer my questions in rhyme,
I'd ask the occasional table
what it was for the rest of the time.

Over

'It simply wasn't meant to be'.
We're meant to say such grown-up things.
Though I loved you, and you loved me,
it simply wasn't meant to be.
We'll smile at our naivety
in time – our talk of vows and rings.
It simply wasn't meant to be;
We're meant to say such grown-up things.

Food Face

A lemon-wedge nose and a broad, ketchup grin;
an oven-chip beard on a porcelain chin;
two carrot-slice eyes and a hat made of cod;
and still you won't eat it, you ungrateful sod.

The Daddy

I don't feel like a proper dad
who understands how engines work
and knows when interest rates are bad
and owns a book about Dunkirk

and doesn't grimace when he drinks
a brandy or a single malt
and doesn't blurt out that he thinks
it's all been someone else's fault

and always hammers nails in straight
and spends his weekends in a fleece
and knows his parents' wedding date
and owns a tin of axle grease

and has a usual at the pub
and knows where roads go from and to
and keeps old washers in a tub
and reads what shares are set to do

and has a blanket in the car
and understands an each-way bet
and knows what anticyclones are
and doesn't have outstanding debt.

And then I wonder if my dad
and all the dads in history
were all just blagging it, and had
the feeling they were frauds, like me.

Norman Wisdom

Oh là là et sacré bleu -
just look at zat poor guy.
E'll never get iz shirt off
wiz zat arrow in iz eye.

Other People's Children

Harry, we're told, is prodigiously bright.
Harry's soprano is *such* a delight.
Harry learns Spanish and Harry plays chess.
Of course Harry's bedroom is never a mess.
Harry read Dickens before he was ten.
Harry's the *victor ludorum* – again!
Whatever he tries, he's magnificent at,
but everyone else thinks that Harry's a twat.

Green Fairy Tale

With every glass her eyes looked bluer,
lips looked redder, hair looked blonder.
Never was a maxim truer:
absinthe makes the heart grow fonder.

The Englishman

The Englishman will no more flinch
if tortured to within an inch
of death by some barbaric foe,
than if he'd stubbed his little toe.
He'll tackle with unruffled ease
a voyage of the Seven Seas,
and clinging to his shipwrecked prow
will scarcely raise a well-groomed brow.

Amid the bloodshed, press and noise
of battle, he retains his poise.
With sanguine mien, he'll tolerate
the subjugation of a state,
or watch with an impassive face
the slaughter of an island race
(all at Her Majesty's behest)
and coolly say it's for the best.

But, heaven knows, he can't abide
the wearing of a hat inside.

Pastoral Poem

Inside my tent, I contemplate
the sky which, leaden, rains and pours,
and can't see what's so bloody great
about the bloody great outdoors.

The Threshold

I turn the key and force the door across
a sliding welcome mat of junk and bills,
the evening sunlight dazzling on the gloss
of skirting-boards and dusty window sills.
A fortnight's worth of trattoria plates,
and linen-shirted strolls, and local wine,
and novels by the pool, evaporates
as all I see is wonderfully mine.
Tomorrow, I must go and fetch the cat,
and mow the lawn, and hang the washing out.
For now, though, well – to hell with all of that!
My favourite chair confirms beyond all doubt,
whatever one professes when in Rome,
that travel's real joy is coming home.

November Haiku

That smell of wood-smoke,
so redolent of autumn.
Shit! The shed's on fire.

Birdsong

Males claim a territory by singing in it,
which tells other males to stay away.
                              BBC Science and Nature

What I, or you,
might well construe
as nature's choral symphony,
your average bird
would claim he'd heard
as: 'Fuck off pal. You're in my tree.'

80,085

As every schoolboy learns with glee,
there is no number greater,
because it spells out 'BOOBS', you see,
on any calculator.

Small Man Syndrome

The moment small men get annoyed,
then everyone starts quoting Freud
and cataloguing, pointedly,
those shorter men from history
(how readily they spring to mind!)
who've been irascibly inclined:
That Josef Stalin, he was short,
and so was Hitler, by report.
Napoleon was really teeny,
as, I'm sure, was Mussolini.
Don't forget old Kim Jong Il -
I've heard that he was smaller still.
Attila Whatshisface – the Hun -
he stood at barely five foot one.
Their meaning's easily construed:
It's down to lack of altitude
and compensatory aggression,
all that violence and oppression.
Anger rises, as a rule,
more quickly in the miniscule.
 I know for now he just seems vexed,
but watch - he'll march on Poland next.

Such unjust slurs make me irate.
They would, of course: I'm five foot eight.

The Couple Upstairs

Their bed springs start to creak;
their ardour has awoken.
That's twice at least this week;
their telly must be broken.

Short Cut

Before you start, can I just say
that, yes, I've booked my holiday
and, yes, I hope it will be nice.
The South of France. We've been there twice.
Still married, yes, and still three kids.
Still working where I always did,
and happy to confirm your views
on any topic in the news,
but couldn't tell you either way
if *Whatshisname* is straight or gay.
The back will look OK as well,
and, no, I won't want any gel.
So, now we've covered all of that
I wonder, could we hold the chat
and I'll just sit here in this chair
while, quietly, you cut my hair?

Anniversary Speech

When love had run its natural course
and lost the spark there had been,
we should have chosen to divorce,
but couldn't face the admin.

The Daily Mirror

A wife may disparage her own face and figure,
lament the extent to which things have got bigger,
more wrinkled or greyer than ever they were;
a husband, however, may never concur.

Casanever

To most men, the notion
of 'romance and mystery'
means clearing the porn from
their Internet history.

The Tide

"Come ladies, gentlemen! Draw near,
and be the first to witness here
before you, on this very stage,
the marvel of the modern age!
A COMPUTATIONAL machine
the likes of which the world's not seen.
It feeds on ELECTRICITY
and – cause of great felicity! -
it does the work, on any day,
of five-and-twenty men, they say!"
All shout "Huzzah!", and shout again -
except for five-and-twenty men.

Thx & rgds

However important you are, or how stressed,
you're never too busy for vowels, I'd suggest.

Armchair Hero

If I'd just practised slightly more
I could have been as good as him.
I'm talented enough, I'm sure;
if I'd just practised slightly more –
and maybe grown to six foot four
and spent more hours in the gym –
if I'd just practised slightly more
I could have been as good as him.

Cold Comfort

Money can't buy happiness,
as people often say,
but misery feels nicer
on a yacht in St. Tropez.

Jake the Peg

Around 1 in 100 is a best estimate of
the prevalence of autism in children.
                    National Autistic Society

Jake's a peg; he doesn't fit:
the world is round, and Jake is square.
He doesn't care a little bit
for toys or games. He likes to sit
and watch his programmes in his chair.
Yes, Jake's a peg. He doesn't fit.
He likes to let dry sand, or grit,
run through his hands, and people stare;
he doesn't care a little bit.
He likes to hold his string and flit
about and sing, quite unaware
that he's a peg that doesn't fit.
And other children might get hit
or sidled past as though not there.
He doesn't care a little bit
when people point, or laugh, or spit;
he doesn't think that life's not fair.
Yes, Jake's a peg. He doesn't fit;
he doesn't care a little bit.

Christmas Circular

Dear friends, another year has passed
and whilst we'd love to gloat
this family has, first to last,
done bugger all of note.

Mothers' Day Deal

You sacrificed your life's best years
in nursing every cold and cough
in cleaning grazes, drying tears
in picking up and dropping off
in making sure we felt no lack
in waiting up for anxious hours
and once a year, to pay you back,
you get some half-dead Esso flowers.

Infamy

for Tom

My son once met a little pig;
they got along just fine.
The piglet said: 'My dad's a boar';
my son said: 'Yes, so's mine'.

Snap

By chance that day you wandered through
the background of my photograph.
I'd gone to Chester via Crewe
by chance that day. You wandered through
my life, and all I ever knew
of yours was, fleetingly, mid-laugh,
by chance that day you wandered through
the background of my photograph.

Two Jars

You know where you are with
both joy and despair;
it's the not knowing which
that it's harder to bear.

Lines for a Godson

for Hector Reece

I can't, I'm afraid, perform magic
or miracles on your behalf.
Life, in the long run, is tragic;
be brave, and remember to laugh.

Sestina

The landlord to'd and fro'd behind the bar,
his knuckles gold, his forearms inked with blue,
dispensing wit and wisdom by the glass
whilst eeking out a half of local Best.
His regulars had all come in tonight,
and most were settled in 'til closing time.

Old Alfred Stokes, who always just had time
for one last half, propped up the public bar.
His body listed more the more the night
wore on, his nose all mottled purple-blue.
He said these days his health was not the best,
and sought to make it true with every glass.

Beside him, just arrived, was Simon Glass.
His cheerful face was flushed; he loved this time
between his mistress and his wife the best,
and humming to himself the final bar
or two of Gershwin's 'Rhapsody in Blue',
he smiled at where he'd heard it twice that night.

The farm lads played the fruit machine all night;
intent upon the wheels behind the glass,
they nudged the buttons flashing red and blue.
They'd surely scoop the jackpot prize this time,
a triple cherry or a triple bar,
and shelled out change, while hoping for the best.

Beside the door sat Mike and Sonia Best,
who'd stayed together since that August night
in nineteen eighty-three in Potters Bar.
She'd had a figure like an hour glass,
but didn't now. She'd tut from time to time
whenever Michael's language got too blue.

As ever, Roger Price was feeling blue.
He said he always tried to do his best,
but seemed to say the wrong thing all the time.
He didn't know where she had gone tonight;
he should have thought of asking Simon Glass.
Instead he bought another chocolate bar.

Beneath the pin-pricked blue of summer night
the place was at its best. Then, sharp as glass,
inside a voice rang out: 'Time at the bar'.

Ode to Joy

The pleasure of one's own success,
however great, could not transcend
that higher form of happiness
which greets the failure of a friend.

21st Century Logic

I'm overweight. I must get slim.
I drive a mile to join the gym.
I run two treadmill-miles and then
I drive a mile back home again.

The Sommelier and Some Liar

Knowledgeable-nonchalant,
I tell the waiter 'Fine'
when really what I'm thinking is
'I'm fairly sure it's wine.'

Remote Possibilities

There are channels for music, and channels for sport,
and channels for things which one probably ought
to refrain from at my age, and channels for news,
and channels for arts and for highbrow reviews,
and channels for films and celebrity chat,
and channels where people buy gadgets and tat,
yet still, without fail, my channel search ends on
the first one I get to with reruns of *Friends* on.

Parental Guidance

'Marry for love, not for money'
was always my mother's advice,
but then she'd add quietly: 'Sonny,
the rich ones can also be nice'.

Half Life

When I was young, I dreamed of adulthood,
of how I'd spend my leisured liberty;
it's not turned out as I supposed it would.

So much of life was not yet understood
but still I felt so sure of what would be,
when I was young and dreamed of adulthood:

I'd go to parties, just because I could,
and watch the sunrise dancing on the sea.
It's not turned out as I supposed it would

when all that lay ahead appeared so good,
and all the stuff I didn't quite foresee
when I was young, and dreamed of adulthood

had yet to show me how things really stood.
The adulthood I saw with certainty
has not turned out as I supposed it would,

and now, of course, I know I never should
have wished away that better part of me
when I was young, and dreamed of adulthood.
It's not turned out as I supposed it would.

Amicable Split

I'm told divorcing needn't be
a source of animosity
between a husband and his spouse
(provided that she keeps the house).

The End of Innocence

Thomas William's tooth was loose, but then disaster struck:
he swallowed it whilst eating jam and bread.
He moped around for days and cursed his jolly rotten luck
'til mother sat him down at last and said:
"The fairy who I claimed would come does not in fact exist;
forgive mama her little peccadillo.
I'll gladly pay a tenner, though, if you would just desist
from defecating underneath your pillow."

Purveyors of the Finest

You never see crests
claiming royal appointment
on pregnancy tests
or on haemorrhoid ointment.

A Game of Soldiers

While some will say: 'Just persevere
and anything can be achieved',
they're all Americans, I fear
and not, alas, to be believed.

Our strength is not tenacity,
if I might speak on Man's behalf:
it's our innate capacity
to say: 'Well, sod this for a laugh',

and failure is just nature's way
of telling us it's time to stop.
When faced with setbacks, run away:
it's how mankind has reached the top.

Stand proud, for evolution favours
not, as Darwin thought, the fit
but you, whose resolution wavers,
noble souls who try, then quit.

An Atheist's Prayer

O, keep me from temptation, Lord above
lest, in my hour of suffering and grief,
the promise of eternal life and love
should undermine my steadfast disbelief.

The Last Noël

Towards the end she used to shop
for everything at Texaco
which on the bus was just one stop,
but still quite far for her to go.

She lived on beans and Ginsters pies
and packs of Fox's Party Rings
and Kipling cakes and Scampi Fries
and Mayfair Menthol Superkings.

That final Christmas, Texaco
provided all her presents too:
for Mum there was some Wash & Go,
for Dad an instant barbecue.

And someone got some cheddar cheese,
and someone else a bag of sticks,
and Grandad got some antifreeze,
although he'd died in '96.

She'd wrapped them all as best she could
in pages from Exchange and Mart,
except the bag of kindling wood.
We smiled, but it broke my heart.

Childhood's Pattern

May I please live my dreams through you,
do all the things I didn't do
when I was young and, shamelessly,
my parents lived their dreams through me?

Clearing

Whilst going through your things, we found,
all packed away so carefully
with tissue-paper wrapped around,
your shoe-boxed memories of me.

Grown-up, with work and everything
there wasn't ever time to come
and stay, or even time to ring;
I'd always send my love through mum.

Now, looking through the cards I'd sent
in childhood, yellowed by the years,
and photographs of summers spent
with you I found the time for tears.

Whatever Happened to Peter and Jane?

Here is Peter. Here is Jane.
How nice to see them both again!
You last met in the seventies
when they were both in dungarees.

Now they've grown up, just like you,
with mortgages and pensions too.
Peter's working in I.T.
and Jane's what's called a 'divorcee'.

Look - can you see Peter's pill?
He worked too hard, and then got ill.
And can you see Jane's Chardonnay?
She drinks a bottle every day!

They've moved away from their home town.
She used to phone when she felt down.
They hardly see each other now.
Their parents died. They had a row.

Remember how they used to play
Through one, unending summer's day?
Where *has* the time gone? Do you know?
It seems so very long ago.

Long Haul

My love is like a clichéd verse:
familiar, but no less true
for that. So much in life gets worse
with time, but happily not you.

Being Frank

And now the end is near for me,
a father, husband, employee,
and through it all, I'm bound to say,
I did it someone else's way.

Masterpiece

Think of all the great, unfinished poems there have been:
Coleridge's *Kubla Khan,* and Spencer's *Faerie Queene;*
Hero and Leander, and *Don Juan*; The *Aeneid;*
The Canterbury Tales. Of course, they're rightfully revered,
and though they're incomplete, they're not in any way diminished,
as often it's the finest works of art which stay un

Acknowledgements

I remain hugely indebted to Luke Wright and everyone at Nasty Little Press for letting me do this.

Special thanks also to Sophie Hannah for her generous support and advice, and to Ben Raudnitz and Daviona Watt for their feedback, proof-reading and lemon and ginger tea.

Thanks, too, to those who have offered support less directly but no less significantly: Judith Aubury, Colin Aubury, Kate Kent, Charlie Bush, Kathleen Geere, Sue Gardner, Claire Cotterill, Joey Patterson-Gordon, Karen Burton and all at the Oundle Bookshop.

Boundless love and thanks to my sons – Fred (for whom I wrote *Jake the Peg*), Jamie and Tom – for giving me ideas, and for helping me to remember that it's important to be a little bit silly from time to time.

Most of all, thanks to Emma Aubury for her astonishing patience, support and good humour.

Also by **NASTY LITTLE PRESS**

Most People Aren't That Happy, Anyway
by John Osborne
ISBN: 978-0-9573000-4-0 | £10

Pub Stuntman
by Tim Clare
ISBN: 978-0-9573000-0-2 | £10

100 Ways To Write Badly Well
by Joel Stickley
ISBN: 978-0-9573000-1-9 | £10

Boring The Arse Off Young People
by Martin Figura
ISBN: 978-0-9563767-3-2 | £5

Mostly Dreich
by Elvis McGonagall
ISBN: 978-0-9573000-2-6 | £5

Arthur
by Martin Figura
ISBN: 978-0-9573000-3-3 | £5

nastylittlepress.org